Corinthian Copper

Corinthian Copper

by Regina Derieva

translation by J. Kates

MARICK PRESS

Library of Congress Cataloguing in Publication Data

CORINTHIAN COPPER
Derieva, Regina
Translator J.Kates
Corinthian Copper.
Poems in English
ISBN: 978-1-934851-28-9
Copyright © by Marick Press, 2010
Design and typesetting by Really Big Robot
Cover design by Really Big Robot
Cover image: Misha Naumcev

Printed and bound in the United States

Marick Press
P.O. Box 36253
Grosse Pointe Farms
Michigan 48236
www.marickpress.com
Mariela Griffor, Publisher
Distributed by spdbooks.org
And Ingram

ACKNOWLEDGMENTS

Some of the translations in this collection have previously appeared in

Artful Dodge, Cyphers, The Dirty Goat, Poetry International, St. Petersburg Review, and in the anthology, *IOU: New Writing on Money* (Concord Free Press)

CONTENTS

ALL THE CONNECTIONS, 1
The age was iron, and rusted . . . , 2
THE RESURRECTION OF LAZARUS, 4
Geography exchanged . . . , 4
The groves race by the train car . . . , 5
With a pine needle, air stitches up a gaping hole . . . , 6
On the terrain of written speech, an excavation . . . , 7
BETWEEN THE WINDOW AND THE DOOR, 8
WINTERTIME LECTURES FOR TERRORISTS, 9
Snow tossed like a subpoena under the door . . . , 24
I have always known . . . , 25
In the book of life to lie like a bookmark . . . , 26
The dead walk . . . , 27
The outsider looks at a star . . . , 28
You struggle . . . , 29
Every trout swims in motherlands . . . , 30
Do not pick up / this stone . . . , 31
You will recognize yourself, and you . . . , 32
Although I don't agree with the majority of your words . . . , 33
The face of an angel is open . . . , 34
EVERYTHING YOU NEED TO KNOW, 35
MARE CLAUSUM, 41
TRAINING IN SILENCE, 45
Black holes in the memory . . . , 48
Look at / how old the mirror . . . , 49
CURATOR AQUARUM, 50

Sometimes / an eclipse of the Sun . . . , 51

Across the sky flew / a pterodactyl . . . , 52

And then rain fell . . . , 53

Argument does not give birth . . . , 54

God stirs together . . . , 56

I work / with Corinthian copper . . . , 57

Every poet . . . , 58

A dead man . . . , 59

The one thing left . . . , 60

At night in other people's homes . . . , 61

There was another street there . . . , 62

In the foreseeable future . . . , 63

The opera of a long winter. . . . , 64

TO WHOM IT MAY CONCERN, 65

Kings love to read . . . , 66

HOW YOU TALK AS YOU APPROACH YOURSELF, 67

SIGNS OF SURVIVAL, 68

JERICHO, 69

AN HONORABLE PROFESSION, 70

ARCHANGENGLAND, 71

from AN ENLARGED WORLD, 82

PROSCOPIA, 84

THE DEPLORABLE REMINDER OF SAMOTHRACE, 85

A CONSISTENT PROPERTY, 86

Translator's note, 87

titles in italics are in their original language

ALL THE CONNECTIONS

What there used to be in earlier times
also got measured in horizons.
Measure of grief, measure of exile
letters from the front, letters from Pontus.

Unroll the prairie like a scroll,
grasshopper, weep over its wide spread.
The stallion may plant his proud hoof,
the horseman's shoulders, heavy with lead.

Closer to the sea does not mean
that the ship — its deck, its mast — is closer,
but nothing stands still, it is time that knits
home to home in the summer resort.

Weeping continues, space in between
stretches out — time is so long.
Wrap the wanderer in royal purple!
Give him a friend, give him a son.

They give him nothing except tears.
They explain, nothing more is allowed.
They open up: This is for you — here's
black bread with Black Sea salt.

The age was iron, and rusted,
completely corroded, like a knife.
with the blunted point of power
that set worlds trembling.

And they carefully clean with sand
the fragment of dull steel,
a terrifying muscle straining
like a primitive lever.

THE RESURRECTION OF LAZARUS

It sounded incredibly strange,
and tender, "Lazarus, come forth."
Out of the whisper and thunder of the World
the dead man stood between his bitter women.

His eyes were opened,
but there was no decay in his eyes,
instead of the destiny of dust and ashes,
the light and flame of transformation.

Geography exchanged
white splotches for black prairies.
Snow fell like sunburn — it is likely
ash will soon sift down from the sky.

And with the final war, the final
sensation of bitter sorrow
I look at the other world from the front line
I beg: Lord, give me the sea.

Give me, Lord, the oceanic sea,
the lacy, salty liquid,
where the soul can linger in peace
and not weep, losing courage.

The groves race by the train car,
not hiding their tears, and stumbling,
there is a skill, like traveling, easier
to live and wait for luck to come.

Let them fly, turning into ribbon
that has wrapped and stifled voice,
indifferent to all argument,
that will bear the speed of a shudder.

Will bear the shaking . . . And a beggar
rides somewhere and somewhere back
whistling in the dark, he is seeking
the compassionate speed of Light.

With a pine needle, air stitches up a gaping hole,
and repairs a seditious sail with the same little needle.
To sail off, you need to swear loyalty to the sky,
you need to fly away, not leave tracks in the clay.

To start singing, you need iodine, salt and ocean,
you need a Greek sail on a pinewood mast.
In a hospital corridor you need to sew up with metal
your beggarly childhood, your destitute old age.

Unstitch the seam between Charybdis and Scylla
using a pinewood hope — and sigh, at last, and weep,
but not over what was left roofless and oceanless,
but only for death from the Tropic of Gloom.

On the terrain of written speech, an excavation:
fragments, potsherds . . . on the terrain of speech
everything seems under control — in quotes, parentheses,
as if the sense were not yet declassified.

As if the thought were not yet disclosed,
as if the introverted vision of the Ogre
did not want to see anything outside,
or be tempted by the horror of the moment.

As if the sphinx, escaping from cunning Greeks,
set such a strange riddle,
that no one anywhere nearby would risk
remaining simply a human being.

No one thirsts for the anonymous life
of a starling, a martin, an aerial password,
of a blood-stained camp and a prickly wound
sustained only by the strength of the poor.

And if it isn't about the field, the page,
or the page that stopped by this field,
then a word keeps and extends the Word,
no thought to tear itself away from pain.

BETWEEN THE WINDOW AND THE DOOR

A different dimension. The advance scout
takes in how a part of speech goes begging
on dry land. How an otherworldly light
of the Homeland lies on outsiders.

How the Lorelei, once across Lethe,
will pose, armed with pistols to the teeth,
for a memorialist and a harpist.
How the streets empty out after a sweep

of the next ism in line. "Twinkle, twinkle
Little Star" the scout thinks, nearly
resigned to prison. Between the door
and the window lives a molting monster.

And if it were not for China and its wall,
the scout could pretend to be a stranger
and exit by either the window or the door.
But there is no land where beasts live in peace.

That's all there is, and any amount of sobbing,
like a nightmare, says nothing about anything.

WINTERTIME LECTURES FOR TERRORISTS

(poems from the narrative "Identity Card")

One summer, at a Black Sea holiday resort, I made the acquaintance of a Middle Eastern terrorist. Like me, he was there to get some rest. Or, like me, he was letting it appear that he was there to get some rest. Thus we were alike in our inability actually to rest and to accommodate ourselves to those around us.

Ten years later, in Jerusalem at the church of Saint Peter, he fell to his knees beside me. I do not know if he was Catholic, but I do know that he, like me, did not have Israeli citizenship. And I know furthermore that he, lacking any citizenship, attached no meaning to this. In this way, too, we were alike, as people. People without a fixed place of residence. Therefore I was not surprised when he suggested that I offer lectures for those of his own kind.

Winter came, an inappropriate time, and I answered him that I would try to write something inappropriate. Inappropriate but deadly.

Strategy

In order to see
the future,
stop staring
at the ground.
Under your feet
are ruins,
shards of glass,
scattered
bones —
all in the past
those that didn't make it.
Under your feet

is ground,
on which
you have to
stand firm.
Stand firm,
in order
not to die
of fear.

Building hiding-places

Orpheus once again
descends into Hell,
deeper
and deeper
descends into Hell,
but he finds
not even a shadow
of Eurydice.
he does not know
that other terrorists
have anticipated him
and not even a shadow
of Eurydice
remains
after the explosion
of a home-made
bomb
assembled outside
Moscow.

Theory of recruiting

Bitchy children
are born
nursing grudges like stones
they hurl
their whole lives long.
The children
of bitchy children
are born
nursing grudges like grenades
in order to blow
everything to pieces
and to leave their descendants
the guts
the still smoking guts
of bitchy children.

Armaments of the enemy

The window used to
have an opening
to stick your head through
to ask angels
passing by
how long it has been
by hour, day, year, century
since the birth of Christ.
A door used to open
onto a balcony,
and cumulus and cirrus

clouds
floated
through the room.
Still earlier
prophets used to meet
on the stair landings.
Quite frequently
prophets used to meet.
But now common sense
has the upperhand.
Finally, common
sense has won,
and we know too well
the other side
of that.

Security services

Something eternally
monstrous stabs
wounds like a splinter
of monstrosity
the unfortunate eye
or ear.
To become G,
you have to give up seeing.
To become B,
you have to give up hearing.
Everything visible
or audible
outside.

Camouflage

The Gorgon Medusa
wearing mirrored dark glasses
from Poland,
blindingly bright, trudges
after the famous act of terrorism
leaning on the shoulder
of a Harvard professor.
Snakes hiss softly
on her
head
become myth and terrestrial
globe.
The myth is what
boils up in salt water
with nettles.
In cold seawater
helpless points of contact
with an earlier terror,
wretched
in the face of everything
not myth.

Exposing surveillance

1

A person collapses
 collapses . . .
  A person collapses
   until
    he falls
     to his knees.
      What remains
       the tower
        appearing
         beyond him?

2.

Poetry has left
 poetry,
  to sleep under a tower,
   which is about
    to fall. Somehow
     they are connected: po-
     etry and tower,
      tower and the person a-
      bandoned by poetry.

3.

You could say that the tower could not endure heaven's look.
You could say that the person chose to know where he was.
You could say that nothing was left of poetry, except the tower and
 the person.
You could say nothing, given that the tower the person and poetry do
 not exist.

Schoolyard battles

A snippet of lead —
a thing perfectly well
understood,
better than
human life.

Capacities for connection

So here
is reality
carried out feet first
by attendants in filthy scrubs.
And here
it comes back again
out of reanimation
in scrubs snatched
from one of the two
attendants.
From the past or
the present,

without hope
of a future.

Recommendations of a general order

The crooked must be made
straight.
That's about it,
only one
mission —
to prepare a straight
path for
ourselves.

Local orientation

From west to east,
from north to south,
from southwest to northeast
and
from eastnorth to westsouth
we go and go and go
and see, if we can,
in a heathery wasteland
on a chalk hill
in the shadow of Shakespeare
in a fog of snow and rain
English
High Gothic
cathedrals
gesturing with their spires.

Diverse cathedrals of the
XII
XV
XVIth
centuries.
They drop from the sky
like waterfalls
or they
reach to the sky
like bonfires,
trees,
waves,
birds.
But no people. No
people — who
have refused
everything.

Revelation of the chief objectives

Looking around, I saw
a shade.
I recognized Vergil
offering me
a *Guidebook to Hell*.
I began to read,
sorting out housing project K,
from district J.
There were a great many
familiar names,
the so-called

front line,
working as usual
the genre of obituary.
"Sauce for the goose, sauce for the gander!"
the vanguard called
in black and white
like an advertising proclamation.
And in a certain
artsy-fartsy café
daily on the menu:
square eggs,
standing for
love.

The study of foreign languages

We believe
in unbelief:
we believe
there is no God.
"No God"
we tell each
other confidently
as if
He Himself
had told us.
Told us and retreated
to a monastery.

Leaps from partway up

A parachute opens
like a butterfly
from Nabokov's own collection.
In principle,
just silk,
a coat-lining, a Russian
flight jacket.
Nothing from above
except earth,
Nothing ever
except earth.
And a stone
shattered by a blow
does not focus our attention
on anything else,
by typesetting.
We will all be turned to dust.

Recommendations of a general order

Learn to read
between the lines.
Learn to read a butterfly
between the lines
of sky,
to understand
what is too hard
to understand.

Reconnaissance

In time
of war
swallows
keep flying,
lilac blooms,
snow
or rain falls,
the sun occasionally
shines,
people are born and die,
serve black coffee
at cafés
in tiny white
demitasse cups,
pray to God,
feed stray
cats,
dogs,
read
the Gospels
in Braille,
lose keys
and find them . . .
In the time
of the six hundred
sixty-sixth
world
war.

Minefield

Everything withdraws,
except the Lord
Jesus Christ.
Everything withdraws
to a safe
distance.
They go away as far
as it is possible to go.
They go away from God,
so that He once again
carries
His cross
on an empty road.

Tactics

Never look
behind.
There, back there,
war
for a hundred, for a thousand years —
simply war.
Do not look back.
There death
dresses up as
Mnemosyne.
There a person
fights to the death
for his right

to be called
mortal.

A message in code

And now, just as before,
it is still necessary
to come and go
to rinse out your mouth,
to clean your ears,
to wait to be
counted,
and also
to wait to be excused,
admitted, allowed to communicate
and also
to run the risk of being
understood,
to wear glasses
with lenses
that obscure
the enemy and many
other things.
And I am now
the conductor of shades,
of elusive, transient
sensations,
and I am now
the link between this
and the other world,
which rolled me

from the moment of my birth,
and yet,
whatever more (The rest is in code.)

Snow tossed like a subpoena under the door,
and there is someone who better hurry up,
if only to cut his losses
on the far side of understanding.

But the noise of horses at his back
and hoofbeats coming on.
and the horror of an icy life
whistles in his shattered mind.

I have always known
the uselessness
of higher mathematics.
This I have always known.
One, two, three . . .
are all a person needs
to count out
the footsteps of death.

In the book of life to lie like a bookmark,
to crawl stubbornly along a single line.
Read sweet where it's written bitter,
insist on straight where there's a turn.

In rust there is fire, water and rock,
in mourning — trees, shrubbery, grass.
A man will flee faster than a deer
from judges, when truth is not there,

from leaders, when eyes are blind,
from the known and from the unknown.
Only an ember pressed to his burning lips
will become his language and his home.

The dead walk
among the living,
looking through the windows
of their eyes,
trying to find
their own reflection.
The leaders of the people
narrow their eyes.
The leaders of the dead
people.

The outsider looks at a star,
his head hurts. There's a party
in the garden, in the garden
small talk just for show.

Nobody needs the prodigal son
of the nation, fallen suddenly into a pit.
How long can you live, all alone?
How long can you wait, pig-headed?

How long live as a poet — night,
morning, day, beginning and end?
A fledgling ought to peck the heavenly light
with its beak of pitchblack winters.

This blue-black-blue, this light
he should love forever.
Saying "yes, yes," or "no, no"
like an Evangelist or a star.

Like a star or an Evangelist
having a particular light in mind, the light of Christ.
Where the tongue of the outcast is pure,
if ready for absence.

You struggle
in a broken zinc washtub,
pumping your gills,
quivering tail,
weeping immense scales,
with round eyes
filled with mother-of-pearl.
Thus deepwater fish
compose among dwellings.
Golden
fish, fulfilling
any wish
at the cost of their own lives.

Every trout swims in motherlands,
every stream flows in birthmarks.
And someone, picked out from notes,
that rang like a bunch of keys,
does not know who he is. The passage
from light to dark, from reality to dream.
And the trout flows with music
from all sides.
And the water called by the trout
is not to be scooped up in hands,
in order not to take up the living trill
and, having slaked thirst, to sleep.

Do not pick up
this stone,
stones like these once
were the death of St. Stephen.
Do not mingle
with this crowd,
once already
it has demanded a Crucifixion.
Everything that once was
over and over again
will be repeated, so that you,
when you come to meet death,
will not send to his death
someone else.

You will recognize yourself, and you
will recognize what will happen quickly.
Just so the recognizable winter
and the city trampled down by it.

Just so the recognizable fate
and the scene chosen by it.
So will the archangel's trumpet
be known like a smidgen of decay.

Although I don't agree with the majority of your words,
all the same I salute you, my enemy, I salute you.
Nobody knew how to express impartially
my own experience and feelings, knowing the shame of the time,
bringing the fear of eternity. Better to clench your teeth
and lie down: No sounds, no figures,
no wretched fantasies, nor rough conclusions,
but the conjunction of distance and height.

The face of an angel is open like
roses or books or distances.
No one among the dead is free of love
and, so, of grief.

To die for the right cause,
in order to avoid a life of metal thorns?
In a rose, which has no boundaries,
an angel smiles wearily.

Let me be within life, God's messenger,
within death let me be, becoming tired,
that, gradually failing, I may revive
to faith and hope.

EVERYTHING YOU NEED TO KNOW

You think this is for you?

No matter how
you look at it,
life is abnormal.

In time and space
you beat your head
against time and space:
Let me out!

A transit prison
from which you
are transported as a package
in stages
of space and time
to an unknown
executioner.

I do not want to live
you cry
and you beat your head
against the masonry
of, perhaps, the Great
Wall of China.

But there was a time
stars lodged
in your eyes.

Where is your home? Where are you going? What are you doing?

You
still exist.
Over there
you exist
somewhere in imagination.
Like the snows
of yesteryear, which
have not
yet melted away.

Teach what you should learn, or learn what you should forget

We lived in an iron age:
In an iron mousetrap
we caught
iron mice,
in an iron cage
we held
iron birds,
we stood everyone
nose in an iron corner
knees on iron peas.
There was a right bed
for the princess
of the pea!
The bed was
iron.
On the iron bed
lay a mattress

in a prison jumpsuit,
you were only just released
from a prison-camp
or jail,
returned
from a lumbering workgang.
Next to the iron mattress
an obligatory
iron mug
with iron water,
and next to that
an iron slice
of bread.
Iron Felix looked down
from the wall
of the iron torture
chamber,
unsatisfied
by the paper icon
and the child of nine
in iron boots
whose tears
rusted the metal.

Because you know yourself

You are always
coming up with new ways
to distract
yourself from
yourself.

For example, you
run your life
off the rails.
For example, you explode
intrusive
truths.
For example, you betray
the state secret
of your existence.
For example, you deracinate
yourself,
your roots, you think,
too primitive.
For example, you put yourself
in prison,
instead of shackles,
for not following orders.
In general, you cleverly,
twisting everything you say,
considering words
your private property.
What you were
was to please yourself
when others
didn't matter.

Do you still believe?

You are
one particular thought
of God,
carried out beyond all limits
of understanding.
An immortal thought.

I know you can brawl

A man got himself lost
in a maze of streets, helplessly
waving his hands. Where am I?
It can happen to you.
Summer pierces his
body with the slanting
rays of the arrows
of Saint Sebastian.
If he stops, his confusion
will tear him apart. What am I?
On unsteady legs, he trails
after his own shadow,
standing as a fingerpost
indicating nothing
but darkness. What time is it?
This has no meaning
for the one who got himself lost.
And rght now you,
spinning out of the orbit of life,
will rip something open

and
explode any connection of names.

Your life is precisely as you wanted it

You are coated with verdigris
like a coin
that has lain in the the earth
for a thousand years.
But nothing will make you new,
not even sandblasting.
And just where will we find
the sand?
It's all in the sundial.
And through my fingers
trickle now
particles of you.
Only a flood
of consciousness stays fresh.

MARE CLAUSUM

Tristis est anima mea

The saints
go where they
are least expected,
where the roads
that lead into
your heart
are long overgrown
with weeds

Per acclamationem

Impossible
to run without stopping
to sleep without stopping
to eat without stopping,
to swim without stopping
to read without stopping
to love without stopping
to think without stopping
How is it then
I am compelled
without stopping
to suffer?

Aqua et igni interdictus

They have expelled me
forbidden the use
of the sources of water,
forbidden me to warm myself
at the shepherds' fires.
It is up to me to gather
within myself
fire and water.
It is up to me to conserve
within myself
fire and tears
enough to last
a thousand years
of exile.

Cognata vocabula rebus

Consciousness also has
its horizon — a thin line
of pursed lips.
This is the frontier where I
am the border-patrol,
guarding my own sanity
from madness.

Abeunt studia in mores

The time has come
to cook up stones
for Chronos to swallow.
Let him gulp them down
thinking he is swallowing
me — a person of evil
character.

Scripta manet

What has been written remains
on the face:
in the eyes,
on the corners of the mouth,
in the wings of the nose,
and at last on the brow,
where your cross
is sketched.

Sunt certi denique fines

In what language
was the herald speaking,
when he appeared where
he was not expected?
In the language of Empire
the herald was speaking,
whom no one understood
and whose head

they drove nails into
to stop him from speaking
and die.
A single rusty
nail I found on the shore,
rusty with blood
and time . . . So why
am I speaking the language
of poetry there,
where I was not
expected? You see,
my head
is more vulnerable than the fifth
illustrious warrior...
But what's done is done
and it's already too late
to change anything in this world —
a world where John the Baptist
was beheaded, and Jesus
Christ crucified . . .
I see Heaven when I look at a plate,
God in a tree.
Congratulate me:
soon
I will be dead!

TRAINING IN SILENCE

Speech is about
something very important.
About something so important,
it calls for not speaking.
Speech is about
stillness.

**

It is forbidden to speak with a person
in a certain language.
It is permitted to be silent with a person
standing upright
as with a hill or
a cathedral.

**

Beginning everything from the beginning
never gets in the way,
even the world
does not hinder a beginning,
if not with the world
to be at one
with God

**

A face screwed up
like the bole of a tree,
in order to mourn
the foliage that flew away.

**

When God weeps,
it rains.
Learn this and you
will shed silent tears.

**

Stone keeps silent,
And Peter keeps silent,
the first Trappist
on Earth.

**

In silence are more
subtleties than in speech,
and much can be read
in the eyes.

**

It is fitting to say farewell
to a little something
that you own,
for the sake of a wish
to own less.

**

On the prairie of your own soul
stands a Trappist, leaning
on the staff of a prayer.
and the soul blossoms.

**

Behind the door there is no
paradise, but that
makes no difference.
And in through the window fly
butterflies of snow.

**

Understanding a silent person
means not speaking
and keeping silence with him,
Recognizing a silent person
means recognizing
the stillness in which
even the flight of an angel
cries out.

**

When you raise questions
but nobody answers you,
do not despair:
stillness itself is
God's response.

FOR TOMAS VENCLOVA

Black holes in the memory — farewell, Mnemosyne.
No one can raise a monument to the past, where
there is nothing but filthy trenches and heavy clay
and the graves of those who wished to walk on water.

Hands used to throwing clods down a terrible void
can no longer hold a weapon or even a stone.
In the kingship of Priam, Troy was burned and destroyed:
Gone the girls and wives, lovers and husbands gone.

As if after a bomb-blast, picking through craters,
I am trying to gather the splinters of shattered speech.
If I could only untangle and straighten the shards:
We need to protect our memories, each from each.

Look at
how old the mirror
reflecting you
has grown.

CURATOR AQUARUM

You see, how in the Roman Empire
everything was wonderfully constructed
so that they even had an official
caretaker of the waters.
I'd like to think that Ovid
wasn't sent into exile,
but commissioned to instruct
the Scythians in classical prosody
and to invent new offices
for the barbarians, who loved
to gaze at the waves
of the Euxine Pontus.

Sometimes
an eclipse of the Sun
sometimes
an eclipse of the mind,
sometimes everything,
maybe even
right now.
Coming to yourself
you don't recognize yourself.
It seems you have to look for
yourself, too,
in some other country,
to begin existence
all over again,
not having learned
to live.

Across the sky flew
a pterodactyl, and everyone
believed in Pterodactylia
and said that faith
in Pterodactylia helped
get them through, find
self-confidence, become
wiser, wealthier,
more handsome, stronger.
Across the sky flew . . .

And then rain fell
from manna, and snow
from manna, and in the sky
not a single cloud
remained. And there was
such intense heat, it was
impossible to breathe, and the ground,
like an old book,
was covered with cracks.
The heat heaped up even
in the wrinkles of leaders,
there was a waste land
inside and outside,
a desert
inside and outside.
But then the rain fell
from manna, in the desert
snow fell from manna.
And the people were filled
with the bread of the Lord
and began to think of turning back
from everything in nature, and began to teach
this to the children, and to reckon
natural sciences, and to secure
that manna is primary, but it
was not necessary to go into the desert . . .
All through that same desert, where the
rain will fall no more, the snow
will fall no more, and heavenly
manna will not fall.

Argument does not give birth
to truth.
Argument gives birth
to the second,
third,
fourth,
and thousand and first
Rome.

In the wall there's a door,
and in the heart,
and in a tree,
and in the sky . . .
Everywhere is full of doors,
which will not open for us.

God stirs together
mud, dust and grit
so that you can see again
and come to know
that a tear
is the very purest product
on earth.

I work
with Corinthian copper,
I use it to make
knicknacks
that I carry
to market, where
nobody buys them.
Nobody buys them,
thinking that the secret
of Corinthian copper
is long
forgotten.

Every poet
has his own
graveyard of verses
where he sometimes
stops by
to leave
a bouquet of cheap flowers
or
a sheaf of airy thoughts
on one of the stones.

A dead man
sailed from the kingdom of the dead
with the coin of the dead in his mouth.
The dead Charon navigated
his dead ferry, walked
through the crowd of the living,
selecting those whom nobody had buried,
and sailed away again
to the Helladic shore
along the avian waves of the Black Sea,
carrying the dead
into a new emigration.

The one thing left
of all my affairs
was to set in front of me
a sheet of paper.
Of all those things that mattered before.
All the rest fell away
and left me alone facing
the miserable square
of a mottled suprematist.
There were no other affairs
waiting for me.
In that other world
where I am now,
people write white on white.
They write love letters
one after another
and tear them up into tiny
tiny, tiny flakes of paper.
And then snow falls.

At night in other people's homes,
having had none of my own
for a long time now, I've
lost my sense of smell.
Lying on other people's beds,
I dream other people's dreams,
from which it's hard
to tear myself away.
My legs are runaway prisoners,
shackled in the stocks of time,
they no longer want to move
along this earth.
There is not even paper
under my hand,
so it happens
that I write in my own heart,
turned inside out.
See, how my heart screeches
all night long on the world's axis ,
turning my face
toward the impossible.

There was another street there,
a street so endless
that no one knew
in whose dreams it began
and in whose it came to an end.
No one knew
when it climbed into the mountains
and when it led downhill.
No one knew
who lived on that street
and who no longer lived there.
No one knew anything at all
or wanted to know,
asked only to be left in peace
on the street of the Prophets,
whose prophecies here
were only mockery.

In the foreseeable future
nothing unforeseeable
is anticipated:
birds cry out in the languages
of dispersed peoples,
dispersed peoples
in the old way
dream about a future
making a better life
for their children.
"Our children will," they say,
"Live otherwise than we
have lived. Our children will . . . "
But the children do not feel
like children, do not feel
like the future, do not feel
unforeseeable. Just what
do the children feel? Ask them,
Ask your own children
yourselves, what they feel
when with their long poles
the daughters of pharoahs
draw willow baskets out of the turbid
waters of time.

The opera of a long winter. A half-tone
lower, frost. The air, modulating flat, cools.
A maple and its spreading, leafless crown.
A recitative, determined by the roles.

How I stammer, how I mix up my dates,
Cue the prompter, how many winters I can
Look forward to. Time, whenever it was,
bundled me off onto too fast a train.

I couldn't find a seat there, the doors
wouldn't close, it stank like a lavatory.
Birds and beasts of prey were the passengers.
Darwin would have enjoyed the menagerie.

The plot lasted so long, was so terrible,
and no talking there about unity.
I was not slain in hand-to-hand battle,
the voice of it all was haggard, hurt.

I no longer need a score or libretto,
the classics, costumes or stage-props
of a deceitful spell and total hell
where one person upstages another.

TO WHOM IT MAY CONCERN

to me, made up of scraps of dreams, of lands
I've never seen, of plain reality,
of air, of salt, of fundamental things
independent of the yeast of time,

of clay and iron, of undulating water
and pebbles kicked up underneath my feet,
of the faith and hope against that wall
where victims wait for execution, turning

into heavenly stone, of quiet and of space,
that a woman passes on from other women,
from desert places, mile after mile
into space where a sense of things is lost,

of whispering, from looking at that object
which humankind has come to label God,
at death itself, which was not and ís not
at life, which will not last for very long.

Kings love to read
about the common people —
woodcutters, bricklayers,
chimney-sweeps, milkmaids . . .
The common people love
to read about kings.
They are eternally interested
in balls and receptions, victories
and defeats at tournaments,
weddings, christenings
and funerals . . . The main thing
that stirs them into life,
the common people and the kings —
are the fantastic histories
of innumerable kings
and common people, in which
every one of them remains
in the place where they belong.

HOW YOU TALK AS YOU APPROACH YOURSELF

Everyone has a past,
in order to look back and say:
I wasn't there.

Everyone has a future,
In order to shrug your shoulders and say:
That won't be me there.

Everyone has a present,
In order to wave it away and say:
That's not me here.

SIGNS OF SURVIVAL

The exclamation mark
of a Koch bacillus,
the comma of cholera.
The deadly syntax
of bacilli mixes into
the life of an organism.
Just in time, relinquish
punctuation marks.
But what to do
if death brings the business
to a full stop.

JERICHO

There is a certain ancient, antique
city, of those who re-enumerated

the legions of Vespasian and Titus,
of those who married and raised children,

of those who sickened and those who died,
of those who made war and commerce,

those who tempting and strutting among themselves,
of those who loved and bickered

of those who grumbled about the present
and those who thirsted for someone's death

all the dumb ones and the prattlers, all
the blind and the clairvoyant. A city

that for a very long time has grown downward
not upward, falling apart

into the atoms and molecules
of a yellow biblical sorrow.

AN HONORABLE PROFESSION

To be a spy in our time is
the most honorable of professions.
A spy earns good money
but for the time being there's just about
no need to do a thing: watch,
remember, and win the confidence
of other spies. In a school
where I was trying to master a new language,
spies from all over the world
were studying with me, pretending that there
was something more they need to know.
As it was, they hung out with each other,
making do without the help of language.
They clarified who works where
and how (à la Mata Hari or
Cooper's Natty Bumppo) incinerating
each other with their glances.

ARCHANGENGLAND

Commentarius perpetuus

1

On and on and on I ride. The road always
begins with a wheel, and with a wheel
finishes up something like Russian
literature. Radishchev traveled
from Petersburg to Moscow, so Anna Karenina
could fall under the wheels of her train.

On and on I ride into England, puzzled
what was it impelled me to travel to England
exactly when I had decided to begin
an epic poem about archangelic annunciations
O Michael, O Gabriel, O Raphael . . . .

On and on I ride through England. An Englishman
in the London-Brighton train sits opposite me
— high-browed, thin-lipped, a Brighton man —
reading a newspaper. A living Englishman
just think of it! The image of Charlie Chaplin.

The conductor cried out, to break your heart,
"Hey, don't even think of missing
your station!" But I was not thinking
of missing anything. Outside the window
cattle and sheep were grazing, bees flying,
big cats creeping (The Sunday Times
had news about a new pack of panthers
and jaguars, let loose by well-wishers

in County Sussex) and I ride, and each station
is for me a final point of arrival.

Voices forge iron, my fellow-traveler
relaxes his lips to smile at me, "Don't worry,
dear, everywhere you go, you're home."

2

From the beginning to the end
and from the end to the beginning
is the same distance, from which it follows
that past and present have a single length.
To go there is the same as to go back,
but the present is right over there,
out the window. That's how I connect to it,
and if it's like that, is it in the past
or in the future? The present is out there
where you are not, because you are only
hurrying to arrive at a farther there.

3

The country has diminished. Turn over
the stones on its beach, turn each
to the other side, look at it attentively:
Who here is a Briton, a Scot, an Angle, a Saxon?

The shore is strewn with the speechless shrieks
of ancient tribes, a few I carry with me.
The ocean casts up more and more

of the stony people, in order to drag them away
into the deeps and return them again to the island.

Everything passes, except England. This island
is washed by love, although the seafoam here
did not give birth to a goddess, but to fog.
The fog gives birth to mystery, the mystery
to madness. Chaadaev, the Russian philosopher,
found his mystery here two centuries ago,
and in Russia this meant an obligation
to go mad. Alongside an old pier,
he used to stroll along leisurely, stoop,
pick up one or another big-eyed stone;
sometimes he tucked it into his coat-pocket,
sometimes he left it in place, so that when
time had passed I could pick it up, too,
having recognized it instantly,
and drop it back here for whoever steps
along this shore after another century or so.

4

This isn't for me and that isn't for me
but who's asking. Soap bubbles break,
they try to crown you with a dunce-cap,
"babies" from all ends of a diminished world
flutter their tongues affectedly in and out.

A Gay Pride parade in the gay capital city. Beardsley
is turning in his grave. A procession storms
under the windows of the Georgian home where he lived

his own innocent childhood, and where I'm spending
a week as the guest of an artist with many children.
Germans from Japan, Japanese from Germany rejoice,
roar, their hands greasy with cod and chips.

The cod takes snapshots as lesbians shower
each other with Coca-Cola. They are groaning:
summer this year is really so hot
steel girders are melting, nothing more to be said.
See how you have to camp it up, to speak in tongues
and cry out in Russian, "Oh shit!"
Good God, This parade crawls into your heart,
glazes your eyes, twists your brain. But here
the regular patrol of fog comes out of the sea
and the raving ones fly off like bats,
they scatter like rats. They're all gone,
and only Merrie Old England is left,
looking me straight in the eye.

5

Outside the window of the three-story house
on Marine Parade rose a parchment moon.
That's how it is in Old England,
where even Shakespeare was moonlike.
Blinds are gathered like the skirt
of a princess eager for a ball. A returning
wind, of course, catches them up.

The ocean breathes so deeply that
there is no way it can ever die. The moon is
very heavy indeed, difficult to read.
Hands grew tired of holding its second volume
full of long, long, overlong thoughts,
like a game of patience. You deal them out,
you deal them out, but they don't come together.

With brief thoughts many things are simpler —
you tied them with laces or with a kerchief
at the throat, and now continue to stare
at the formal portrait of the moon,
under which all of England
all ten million heads of it, that all these years
have not fallen under the axe.

The horizontality of England allows it
to form perfect horizons, and therefore
an Englishman always and everywhere remains
an Englishman. The thoughts of an Englishman
blossom like the garden he weeds
every day, the eyes of an Englishman
are innocent forget-me-nots or pansies.
But flowers ought to be protected, and, lo,
look at all those fences. Look into the eyes
of an Englishman: do you see yourself in there?

Of course, you'll not find yourself there.
The Englishman is an impregnable tower,
surrounded by a deep moat, filled to the rim
with the bodies of the enemies of Merrie

Old England, which has deposited in every
back alley of the world its own last word.

6

Make it your rule to pray on the road to angelic
powers, and you'll find them everywhere. Michael
defends against malice, Gabriel sends good news,
and Raphael accompanies travelers. Raphael?
he's a convivial chap always ready with a joke.

See the archangel Raphael standing two steps
away from me at the bus stop
in a tweed jacket, absolutely essential
for a journey from Brighton to London.
I have a bag in my hands, he has my life in his,
he'll answer for it. The tweed jacket in ninety-
degree weather undoubtedly bothers him. But
in England even archangels look like gentlemen
and consider Leontiev's cry against the harm
jackets do to a nation to be a useless rant. So
in his own jacket and pressed trousers
Raphael engages the driver's interest. "Does this
bus go to Stockholm?" "Of course,
it does, but not today," answers the driver
(also an angel) "Wait a week. Today
it runs only as an express to London."

7

Oaks, chestnuts, beeches, maples,
dogrose, honeysuckle, anemones,
roses, peonies, golden globes . . .
Indians, Pakistanis, Chinese, Kurds,
all without exception in informal
bathing suits and hats with pheasant feathers.
Americans from all the prairies, Arabs
from all the deserts, Asiatics from all
the steppes, Russians from all the forests and
alleyways. Languages, accents, dialects,
jargons . . . Skull-caps, turbans, fancy hats,
yashmaks, dresses . . . Rozanov, another of those
Russian crazies, oversimplified
Slavic philosophy, tore off its
orthodox dress, drowned it in a mikvah.
They never got near English philosophy! . . .
Synagogues, mosques, taj-mahals, cathedrals
entwine each face in a spiderweb of time.
Historical, antihistorical, cultural and counter-cultural
monuments sprout out of the earth
like poets. Only that quartet of Liverpudlians
flying everywhere you will not meet them:
Beyond the endless breakfast, on the cut
lawn, on the banks of the Thames, laundering
money, or in the market. English goods
are always expensive, especially in Russia. There
already during the Crimean War
it was being said: "Oh, what a marvelous coat, it
must be English cloth." English birds

are also expensive, at least their eggs are. They lay
eggs, we collect from them collections
of impressions. Impressions of an island
bigger than the world, an island that swallowed the world.
Saris, tuxedos, topless, frock-coats . . .
Acquaintances, encounters, separations, deaths. . .

Who has not been looking for you, England,
who has not discovered you. Here I am
tossed onto your island like a brand-new
Robinson, not waiting around for a Friday.
My artist friend has excused himself from this role —
he was preparing to die. I persuade him:
Don't die yet, friend, you'll get there, you still have to
lay out three gardens, beget three children
and, finally, paint three archangels.

8

The cries of seagulls (what I call seagulls, I'm corrected,
are cormorants) the howling of children, honking of cars,
barking of dogs, the knock of a pebble, a wave laughing and
music, music . . . People are taking it easy, you know, they eat,
you know, they drink beer, they quarrel among
themselves, like seagulls, for no reason fighting over
a greasy pizza box. I'm fed up with you,
fuck off, I'm the one fed up, fuck off. From the sea
emerge two Russian hitmen, clothed, you know:
black suits, black ties, black eyeglasses,
in their hands black shoes, matching everything else.

They will not kill me, they won't, I don't matter to them,
they have come to kill England. There are more Russians
here than English, among them Herzen, Dostoevsky,
and Lenin. They roam Brighton, they stroll around
London, they observe the Royal Pavilion and
the Millennium Dome, they draw conclusions. Russians,
promptly monitored by not so secret services,
draw conclusions more quickly than others do.
What's good, what's bad? The reference points are lost.

Words are only noise, to which the organ of hearing
is nearly indifferent. The knock of balls, the siren
of ambulances, the clatter of heels, the roar of a pair of airplanes
reading the sky in Braille, the rustle of The Times
and the wrappers of Brighton fruit-drops. The ear
Takes in all of this, except words. Another couple of Russians
light a fire on the beach and bake a potato.
They're laughing while they do this. Tomorrow the sea in this
place will be Black. How many years will it take
to wash away the tracks of this primitive bivouac
of a Russian who has read Dostoevsky and has come to kill
Merrie Old England. The artist whose guest I am
worships Keats and the little garden of Mrs Garnet.

He likes to say: "You, Russians have a lot to be proud of." Oh,
yeah, I'm proud that I gathered together so many pebbles
on the beach. It's not yet time to cast them away. The artist
lives alone, fears the Internal Revenue, old age
and death. I promise him a long life without misery.
I admire that person who is not fed up with speaking
words. Once or twice a day he disappears somewhere,

like the mystical lion of Nottingham, but invariably
he appears again in the evening, holding forth on Brancusi,
Turner or Michelangelo, according to the weather.

9

Russians confirm their brotherhood not by blood, but only
in talk, laying out all there is to know about themselves,
answering each other without waiting for questions.
For such a Russian something always seems, appears,
he recalls, believes in something ... Especially in England.
Especally at 3 Powis Gardens. O Michael, O Gabriel,
O Raphael, ... O Daniel .... From the archangels to the meekest
prophet, from the prophet to the translator to the poet
who lives uneasily with his own Russian wife
near the Greek Church of St. Michael.

However, Russians, like other people, usually
travel the world to look at mountains and rivers,
bridges and piazzas, gryphons and lions, convinced
that they have seen it all. But me, I travel, when I do so,
not in order to get to a place, but to go away.
How quickly I abandoned the shore of "Foggy
Albion," but not alone — in the company of excellent
guides, all of us journeying together to Sweden.

10

The dry kisses of affected gays
gushing their happiness behind my back,
perforate the air as we leave the capital.

Thousands of images outside the window of the morning bus
hurrying on its way to the airport
glimmer with alien dreams.
The field dives behind the woody hedges, to
get lost in the combed fog.
Envying fate, you breathe in
inhaling the naive countryside. From behind,
Sodom calls to Gomorrah "hey, baby!"
No, you do not wish them the fate of Stalingrad,
but you yourself are in no hurry to turn
into Lot's wife. And so you struggle,
as always when you try to stay on your own,
with the noiseless contemplation of prophecies
fanned by the wings of archangels.

August 2003-October 2004

from AN ENLARGED WORLD

1

One of his feet was planted on the right bank
the other on the left (The right did not know
what the left wanted) and between them
sailed vessels which also
could not decide which foot was right,
and therefore suffered shipwrecks
one after another.
That was the reputation of the Colossus of Rhodes,
the sixth wonder of the world.
The world was smaller then, of course,
and there were enough wonders for everyone.
But then the world grew hectic
enlarged by the sum of geographic
discoveries, so that all the more rapidly
it diminished, the price of discovery teeth
set on edge, leaving behind only nostalgia
for a wonder in the hearts of lost colossi.

2

I saw a double rainbow
plucking Minerva out
of the brow of Jupiter
and Athena from the skull of Zeus.
They promised a double joy.
does this mean I'll be able to buy
not only a winter coat, but boots?

3

I stopped by the store
for a loaf of bread,
I gave the cashier
ready money from Atlantis,
but he refused to issue a receipt,
took back my daily bread
and threatened me with the police.
I stopped by the shop next door
to buy myself an umbrella
as a protection from boorishness.
I offered the shopgirl
a crumpled banknote from Atlantis,
but she broke the umbrella
and promised to have me
taken off to jail.
Then I stood on the corner
of the busiest streets
leading into the future,
with a sign, "Donate
to a refugee from Atlantis!"
but the box at my feet
filled slowly up
without a single dollar, without a pound,
a ruble, without a single crown,
but only the currency of Avalon,
Ultima Thule, Shambala and Eldorado,
interesting not even to coin collectors,
who flourished proof that these countries
did not exist.

PROSCOPIA

All morning I worked on a poem
about insects, but I had not finished
it, when I left off to go shopping
to buy something for dinner. Home again,
I went back to my desk, and saw there
in place of my overscribbled page
a live butterfly with the face of Issa
and open wings on which in hieroglyphics
this poem was written.

THE DEPLORABLE REMINDER OF SAMOTHRACE

(which follows the removal from the covers of textbooks in order to avoid the usual mutilation)

Here stands stone Nike
of whom nothing remains
but the heavy wings on her shoulders.
This crippled woman stands
missing her hands and her head
to remind us
of the cost of any victory.

A CONSISTENT PROPERTY

Rising prices do not increase the value
of conscious existence, no.
Paying debts and lamenting
expenses, we can not buy even
a single smidgen of consciousness
to augment what we already have, no.
We are awarded only what
there is, and don't you expect anything more.....
Really now?
The consciousness we have been issued
so quickly passes, melts away,
evaporates, until nothing
at all remains, no.
Consciousness is the constant
denial of the denial of life,
its final page.

Translator's note

Reader, we are perhaps closer than you think.

Regina Derieva the poet exists for me only as she exists for most of you who hold this — as words on a page. I have not met her. The experience that likely separates us is my familiarity with her original Russian words.

Some of these poems have also been translated by others. For the most part, I read those others only after I had made my own versions. Another poet's reading, however, can help a translator correct a mistake or refine a nuance, and I've been helped in my reading of "Archangengland" by the independent translation of Derieva's friend, Daniel Weissbort. A few of these poems have also been run through the fine mill of our Boston area translators' group I nickname the Club Dolet.

Because this book does not reproduce the original texts, I'd like to alert you to a couple of things. First, many of the poems are written in strict rhyme and meter which I have not necessarily carried over into English, lest the poems sound more old-fashioned and formal than they are in Russian; still, I have tried to convey the play and density of the original language. Second, in a couple of places I have translated culture as well as words. In "On the terrain of written speech," for instance, I have substituted the generalized "Ogre" for a specific character (Viy) out of a Gogol horror-story, and in "Between the Window and the Door" I have used the recognizable "Twinkle, Twinkle, Little Star" in place of a Russian verse. The reader who does have the opportunity to read the original (and I hope this selection spurs such an interest) will be able to winkle out other examples. And last, because these translations have been made in consultation with the poet's husband, who acts as her agent and understands English, in places he has communicated the writer's drift along with her literal meaning, and I have privileged the intention over the word. In general, I am immensely grateful to Alexander

Deriev for his generous guidance in my translating his wife's work. It was Alexander who introduced me to Regina Derieva's poems, and in the process of translating I have come to like them more and more.

Reader, I wish you a parallel experience.

www.ingramcontent.com/pod-product-compliance
Lightning Source LLC
LaVergne TN
LVHW011428080426
835512LV00005B/328